The Knight Light

by
Babs Bell Hajdusiewicz
illustrated by
Gregory Nemec

Scott Foresman

Editorial Offices: Glenview, Illinois • New York, New York
Sales Offices: Reading, Massachusetts • Duluth, Georgia
Glenview, Illinois • Carrollton, Texas • Menlo Park, California

"Look what I can do!" said Anne.
"I'm a big bird! Watch me fly!"

"Stop it! You are scaring me!"
said her young brother. "I saw
eight crows on the road today. I
was scared of those big birds!"

"Shadows are scary at night!"
John said.

"Don't be silly, John! We are not
on the road now. We are inside the
castle. There are no big birds in
here. And shadows can't hurt you."

"But they still scare me!" he said.

"Just close your eyes," said Anne.
"Then you will not see them."

Anne saw the full moon outside.
That meant there would be shadows
tonight—in her room!

"John is right," Anne said.
"Shadows are scary at night."

Anne tried to close her eyes. But a giant danced on the castle wall. And birds flew across her ceiling.

"Shadows can't hurt me," she said softly. "I will just close my eyes."

John's scream woke Anne in the
night. "Anne!" he cried.

Anne jumped out of bed. A giant
was at the door. "It's just a shadow,"
she said softly. "Shadows can't
hurt me."

Anne opened the door. She
looked down the hall. Something
moved on the wall! Scary things
raced across the ceiling.

"Anne!" cried her brother.

Anne heard her heart beating loudly. Her feet would not move. "They are just shadows," she whispered. "They can't hurt me. I have to help John."

Looking up, Anne walked along
the hall. "They are just shadows,"
she said. "They can't hurt me."

"I made it!" Anne cried. But then she saw a new shadow. And she saw a light!

"That is a knight's armor," she said. "It can't hurt me. The moon is shining on it!"

"Anne! " said John. "I saw a giant! I'm scared!"

"They are just shadows, John. They can't hurt you. Just close your eyes. Then you will not see them."

"Light a candle, Anne! Light eight candles!"

"We are too young to light candles, John. It's not safe."

Anne thought for a minute.
"John," she said. "We can make a
night light!"

Anne pulled the mirror across
the room.

"Look, John! The mirror helps the moonlight come in the castle. Now you have a knight light!"